Your 60 Minute Lean Business

TPM
Total Productive Maintenance

Your 60 Minute Lean Business
Total Productive Maintenance
May 2012
First Edition

www.lulu.com
ISBN: 978-1-105-76325-0
Copyright © 2012 Jason Tisbury
978-1-105-76325-0

Also by Jason Tisbury:

Your 60 Minute Lean Business:
5S Implementation Guide

7 Steps To A Lean Business

Pocket Happiness

Contents

Foreword

Welcome to the 60 Minute Lean Business series of books. Why 60 minutes? Well for a couple of reasons. It occurred to me a number of years ago while searching through libraries and book stores for texts on the topic of lean manufacturing and lean business that most of the available books were quite large and often not easy to understand for someone new to the topic. The essence of lean is to remove waste from a business and its processes, yet here were all of these books that were filled with non-essential words – waste. I felt a book on the topic of lean should itself be lean. With this in mind I went about writing my first book on lean – 7 Steps To A Lean Business – an overview of lean manufacturing and lean business systems. At 140 pages, this book can be read in a couple of hours and while the details may not enable one to immediately turn a business lean, I believe 7 Steps does provide a very sound overview and entry learning for the lean newcomer.

Now it is time to share the details of some of the different lean tools, I started writing a book detailing all of the tools but soon realised what I was writing wasn't lean enough. And so the Lean Business in 60 Minutes idea was conceived. Your 60 Minute Lean Business – 5S Implementation Guide was the first release borne from this idea. Now the library continues to grow.

If you are a business owner or manager and are looking for a concise, detailed guide to Total Productive Maintenance (TPM), then this book was written especially for you. My goal is to share what I have been lucky enough to learn with other like minded people who may not have had the dumb luck that I have had. When I say dumb luck, I mean dumb luck. The following is the story of how I came to learn lean, I'm sharing this story to firstly build my credentials and secondly to show how anybody can learn and implement these tools.

At the age of 32 I was working in a factory after a recent business failure when I was lucky enough to break two fingers in a ten ton press. It was quite a bad break, twelve months recovery including two surgeries (one bone graft). Now it may seem strange to call that lucky, but luck is what you make of a situation. Even though I had only one working hand, I could still use a computer, and I was fairly handy on a computer (pun not intended). I ended up working with the Quality Manager who by chance was starting to implement some lean manufacturing / continuous improvement ideas in the business. I learnt a great deal during this time. I was also lucky that this company was in the automotive industry and that one of their main customers was Toyota, probably the best company in the world to learn from. I spent the next five years living and breathing the Toyota Production System (TPS) with direct instruction and mentoring through Toyota. Now after having implemented lean systems and tools through a variety of companies in many organisations in many diverse industries, it is time to share what I have learnt for others to benefit.

What is TPM – Philosophy

TPM or Total Productive Maintenance is an asset management system that takes an holistic view of equipment maintenance to ensure a process (manufacturing or business) realises the highest possible level of uptime or availability. There are other systems used to achieve similar outcomes. The most popular two are:

- Preventive maintenance programs

- Overall Equipment Effectiveness (this is more of a measurement than a system)

Both of these lack the lean philosophy or mindset (culture) and therefore do not easily create or align with the other lean tools as well as TPM can. One of the greatest benefits a lean business system will bring to your organisation is the cultural shift that will occur automatically if your system is designed well and implemented effectively. The more lean tools you include in your system the greater effect the culture shift will have and the faster it can be noticed.

Many of the lean tools are designed to measure, analyse and improve a process. TPM, like 5S is designed to maintain the effectiveness and repeatability of the same process. The reason the first two books in this series are 5S and TPM is because these should be implemented before the other tools. Now this may seem strange, as the other tools can help provide faster improvements – true. However without 5S and TPM these improvements may be short lived and difficult to sustain. This is depicted in the Lean House diagram.

Lean Business

Jidoka – Quality

Just In Time

Standardised Work	Kaizen
5S	TPM

Saying all of that, TPM can provide the following benefits:

- Increased machine availability
- Increased uptime
  - This is different to availability
  - Uptime can only be increased if the machine is loaded above the current availability and is therefore a bottleneck
- Reduced maintenance and operating costs
- Increased empowerment and engagement of staff
- Increased asset life
- Greater utilisation of labour
- Greater amortisation of fixed costs
- Increased employee engagement and satisfaction
- Improved production quality
- Improved safety performance

The costs and benefits of maintenance is often restricted to plant and machinery in a manufacturing environment. There is no reason this restriction cannot be lifted and TPM applied to warehousing, service, educational, healthcare operations and many more. Although the capital investment for plant and equipment in a manufacturing business is likely to be higher than many other business types (health being the obvious exception), these costs should be relative to the returns. Saying that, many of the examples used in this book will focus on a manufacturing situation; this is due to the ease of application and explanation.

Simply put TPM is a system of plant and equipment maintenance that enables the highest level of machine availability to support the operational requirements. The desired outcome is to ensure all plant and equipment is available whenever required to satisfy the business requirements.

- If this is in a manufacturing environment, this would mean all machinery and tooling is available to support the production plan.

- In a warehousing and logistics environment, this would mean all material handling and packaging equipment etc. This would also extend to the order management systems (IT).

- In a service industry environment, this would mean all tools of trade, IT etc.

If at any time your business encounters unplanned downtime, your maintenance system is letting you down and costing you money. These costs are not limited to money outlaid to repair and maintain but also money in lost income and non-utilised wages and fixed costs. These hidden costs are often far greater than the actual costs of repair. Many organisations do not measure this accurately; this makes building a business case more difficult.

An effective TPM system will also assist in reducing your overall maintenance costs. When your plant and equipment is properly maintained, even your planned downtime will be reduced and the costs incurred during the planned downtime will be reduced as fewer repairs will be required during the servicing. Add to this the reduced requirement to pay for overtime labour and out of hours for external providers and the true costs of poorly managed maintenance add up.

What TPM isn't!

Firstly, TPM should not be confused with Preventive Maintenance (PM) PM itself is a useful tool and as the name suggests is focussed on preventing machine breakdowns. This is achieved by regular service checks and upkeep. These are generally performed by the machine operators. This both prevents breakdowns and ensures the operators are constantly aware of the machine condition to allow for early detection of problems. This will discussed in detail later in the book.

TPM is also not OEE (Overall Equipment Effectiveness). As the name suggests, OEE is a measurement system employed to monitor the effectiveness of the equipment. In other words, the system measures the uptime, availability, efficiency and quality of the plant. OEE is a valuable management tool used for analysis of the plant and equipment, however it is also useful for measuring the effectiveness of a preventive maintenance or Total Productive Maintenance system. So if we look at this through a Business Excellence view; Management is the Driver; TPM is the Enabler; and OEE provides the results (through measurement and monitoring).

How does TPM fit with Lean?

A Lean Business System combines the benefits of many tools to enable an efficient and effective organisation. To become a best practice organisation you require more than just the tools; you will have to embed a positive continuous improvement culture throughout all levels of the organisation. By implementing a effective TPM system into your organisation, you not only realise the tangible benefits; there are many intangible or cultural benefits that can be attributed to TPM and other lean tools. The beauty of lean isn't actually the reduced operating costs – the real benefits are the learnings and growth of the individuals and the greater organisation along the way.

More information on this topic can be read in Your Lean Business in 60 Minutes – Lean Philosophy or 7 Steps To A Lean Business.

1 – Taking Stock

As the name suggests, this chapter is about identifying where we currently are. Do you have a comprehensive asset register of all plant, machinery, equipment, tooling, tools?

Firstly, what is the difference between plant, machinery, equipment, tooling, tools?

Plant – The necessary infrastructure to support the operations

- Buildings

- Air-conditioning

- Plumbing

- Electrical supply

- Gas supply

- Lighting etc

- Amenities

This list can be quite large but I think from the above you should understand the meaning.

Machinery – Large (usually powered) machines used the business operations. It is often described as bolted down equipment – although this is not always the case. Examples of machinery in a manufacturing plant include:

- Presses

- Conveyor systems

- Assembly robots
- Welding robots
- Laser / turret punch

Once again this list could be very long as every business has different machinery requirements but I think you should get the idea.

Equipment – This is often inter-used with machinery, however equipment is more the larger machines used to support the operations (machinery being used to undertake the operations).

- Packaging systems
- Transportation systems

Tooling – This refers to dies and the like used in machinery.

Tools – These are small mobile tools and machinery used to undertake and support the operations.

In the interests of not wasting words, I will be referring to all of the above simply as 'equipment'.

So, do you have the register? Many businesses do not have a list at all let alone a comprehensive one. If not, this is the first action you need to undertake.

There are many software applications available for this purpose ranging from the expensive, offering extensive capabilities to those that are free and offer far reduced capabilities. You can also make your own spreadsheet or database to capture and manage to your needs. The choice is yours. I would suggest getting the best you can afford as the higher capabilities will be helpful as your program matures. Initially though, a simple spreadsheet is quite sufficient to capture your register.

My advice is to begin with the larger plant and move your way down through the machinery, equipment, tooling and tools. Capture as much information as possible;

- Manufacturer
- Year of manufacture
- Model
- Modifications
- Accessories
- Condition report

The above is the absolute minimum requirement for information. Try and also identify the following:

- Current availability
- Current uptime/downtime
- Service history

The condition report can be categorised into three or four conditions as required rather than a detailed report at this stage. This is primarily for you to understand where you currently sit with regards to your equipment.

Current availability may not be easily attained at this stage if you have not been measuring OEE or similar data. If this is not available a good estimate will be sufficient. This will be important in the next steps in the process. The same applies for current uptime and current downtime. A good estimate is fine in the absence of data at this stage.

Enter all of this information into your spreadsheet or database. This may seem like a lot of work; however it is critical this information is collected. At the very least you now have an inventory of everything for insurance and accounting purposes. If you use some of the items for more than one process or product, it is a good idea to add a column or two to capture this also. The more information you capture early in any initiative or activity, the better results you will have.

While it isn't absolutely necessary, it can be useful to allocate an asset number to each item on your list. This can be useful for identifying your machines by number rather than by name/brand/manufacturer; you may have more than one machine of the same manufacturer. Rather than a metal tag on the body, a plastic tag can easily be applied to the power cable. If you can also record the serial number on the tag and on the database, this will also assist with insurance documentation.

Even if you don't follow the next steps and simply maintain your data as your equipment is serviced you will now be in a stronger position to manage your equipment and reduce your servicing costs. TPM can however provide much, much more than just a servicing schedule and history as you will realise in the following steps.

As with all of the Lean tools, by following the Plan Do Check Act cycle (PDCA) you will realise better and more consistent results.

Plan – Analyse what has gone wrong? Find a gap and make a plan to implement countermeasures.

Do – Trial the countermeasure.

Check – Measure the outcomes from the trial to determine the effectiveness.

Act – If the countermeasures provide the desired outcomes – implement on a larger scale and share the lessons learnt. Otherwise develop new countermeasures and return to Do.

This step is the first stage of planning your TPM program, in essence this entire guide focuses on the planning of your program. However when executing step three we will be following the PDCA cycle closely for each piece of equipment while getting to know your equipment.

2 - Prioritise your plant

The next step is to prioritise all of the equipment. Prioritise all plant, equipment and machinery with the following criteria:

- Reliance – How much does the operation of your business rely on this piece of equipment?
  - Can your business function without this piece of equipment?
  - Is this a primary or subsidiary piece of equipment?

- Contingencies – What contingencies plans are in place if the machinery breaks down?
  - Can you easily outsource or modify the process?
  - Can you substitute the process or equipment?
  - Are replacement parts easily available and accessible locally?
  - Are the skills to repair available locally?

Table the results into a simple two axis chart to rank your plant, equipment and machinery A, B, C, D. See below.

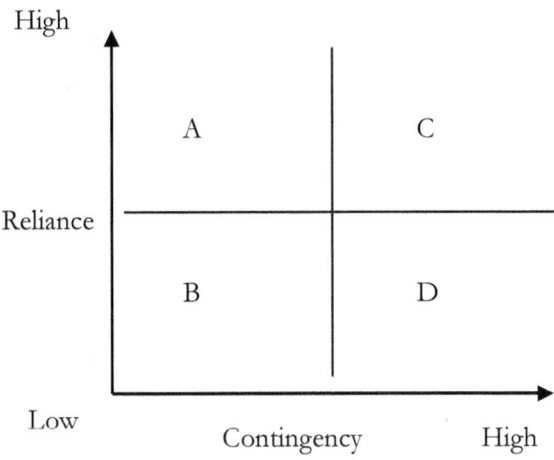

As the above diagram shows, those with high reliance and low contingency will be ranked highest (A); while those with low reliance and high contingency will be ranked lowest (D). There is plausible argument that B and C could be swapped – realistically, it is of little consequence which way you go with this. The key outcome from this is to identify your category A items.

Once you have prioritised all of your equipment, add this data to your asset register; if you're using an asset management application there should be an input field for this, however if you're using a spreadsheet an extra column will need to be added. Sorting can now be performed by priority.

This information will become critical when we come to scheduling the workload in a later chapter. This information is not only important for the purposes of developing your TPM system, it will also be helpful for many other lean initiatives you may embark on in the future.

3 – Know Your Plant

Now you have a complete list of your equipment and have prioritised it you will know which equipment is the most important to keep operational. The higher priority the equipment the more thorough you will need to know it. The better you know the equipment the faster and more efficiently maintenance and repairs can be carried out.

Depending on the size of your organisation, you may have a team of maintenance engineers, fitters and tradesmen or you may have no specialised or dedicated maintenance staff. The term 'you' in these pages refers to whoever is responsible for the maintenance or condition of the equipment in the organisation. Remember, equipment can be manufacturing, office, warehousing or even laboratory equipment or tools.

So how do you get to know your equipment? A good place to start is to read and understand the manuals. Do you even have all of the manuals for all of your equipment? If not, then the starting point is to locate or replace them. These manuals may list all of the operating and preventive maintenance requirements with schedules and specifications. This information should be added to the spreadsheet or data base you created earlier to create a maintenance requirement database.

Add to this a list of all of the consumables for the equipment along with the serviceable hours for the consumables. This information will be useful in step 4.

Some manufacturing plants around the world (specifically some Toyota plants) are employing a very different method for knowing their equipment. In this method, all high priority plant and equipment is totally dismantled and reassembled by the person or team responsible for the maintenance, repairs and general upkeep of the equipment. This is often performed even before commissioning of new equipment. For older or existing equipment, this occurs during a shutdown or, in the absence of a shutdown period an alternative processing method is employed to free up the equipment. This may seem like an extreme measure to take, however the results they are achieving are proving worthwhile.

For this method to be effective it is necessary to totally dismantle the equipment to its component form. This is to enable a high level of knowledge of the equipment. By utilising this method, your organisation will gain a thorough knowledge of its equipment; this will pay off with more efficient and effective maintenance and repair operations.

This is not the only way to get to know your equipment; by structuring maintenance teams to regularly work on the same equipment, you will, over time, create a strong knowledge. This when coupled with the information gathered from the manuals earlier in this step can combine to provide an effective working knowledge base.

Another effective method is to retain parts that are replaced when worn or damaged and later dismantle these to either refurbish for reuse or to gain a better working understanding of the parts and their connection with the larger equipment. While this method can take longer to gain a thorough understanding, the resulting knowledge and understanding can be effective in reducing overall maintenance and repair costs and the associated downtime.

Which ever method or methods you decide to employ it is important to maintain a focus on the reasons for following this step. A strong understanding and knowledge of your equipment will provide the following benefits:

- Reduced planned downtime by reducing the necessary scheduled maintenance time. This is due to the knowledge of parts, wear rates and weak points.

- Reduced unplanned downtime through faster identification of failure causes and more efficient repair works.

- Increased safety through reduction in hazards.

- Increased productivity and reduced operating costs brought around by all of the above.

The above is by no means an extensive list of benefits, but should give you some reasons why this step should be followed. A TPM program can be developed and can be quite effective without following this example from Toyota, in fact most of the effective TPM programs in use in organisations now will not follow the method, often because they simply haven't heard of it. Also, it would be silly to blindly follow this method purely because some Toyota plants have implemented it. This needs to be judged by you and your management team to ensure the system and program you develop and implement has the right balance for your organisation.

4 – Setting up the System

Finally, we can start doing something with the information we have collected. Now there are many software solutions that you can purchase to manage your assets ranging from well under $1000 to many tens and even hundreds of thousands of dollars. If you have the need and resources (capital and dedicated staffing) to purchase one of these systems then I'd recommend you do. However if you are a smaller enterprise and do not have the resources to justify one of purchased systems the good news is you can do just as good a job with a simple spreadsheet and a little time invested.

If you're worried about your spreadsheet skills just go to www.mrexcel.com this site has heaps of free information and tutorials on Microsoft Excel.

You have all of the information you collected earlier, with a few formulas and maybe a macro or two this can be transformed into a TPM system. So what make a TPM system?

According to dictionary.com "a system is a coordinated body of methods or a scheme or plan of procedure." In this context a system is what makes the difference between maintaining and repairing your equipment and implementing a sustainable TPM program. Anyone can and everyone will repair and maintain (to some extent) there equipment, however only those who implement a system will realise the benefits. This is the same for every lean / quality / business tool. I often hear "we've done all of this before" and it is usually true. Often the reason why "it" didn't work in the past was because it wasn't backed up by a system of any kind let alone a successful and sustained system.

So what are the key elements of a good system?

- It must have a documented process that can be followed; this process should be regularly reviewed or tested to ensure it remains effective.

- Responsibilities must be clearly defined.

- It must be measurable; in order to be measurable it must have deliverables e.g. outputs – what and when.

- It must have targets set.

- It must be managed – those responsible must be held accountable.

Two of the biggest and most common failings I see in the organisations I work with are the lack of accountability and a lack of effective performance measurement. Performance measurement should not be confused with performance management. Performance management is what happens when performance measurement either hasn't been effective or has identified a gap or failing in performance. In order to measure performance effectively, it is critical to set up the system or plan effectively.

By spending time developing a high quality plan (at any level of the organisation) you will be giving yourself the best opportunity to deliver in the future. Too much rush through the planning stages and later complain they spend excessive time "putting out fires"; this can be eliminated through effective planning. Quite often it takes a leap of faith before this paradigm shift occurs and the realisation of how effective this can be.

It should be clear by now that without a system, you cannot have TPM. The first step is to develop the process. This book is not a detailed guide to process development so I won't go into great details. If your organisation has a corporate process, procedure or SOP template then utilise those otherwise a simple flowchart will do the job. The key to a good flowchart is the decision points. Make sure all decisions are included and more importantly the effects of the decisions are charted. A good test for a process or flowchart is to give it to someone with no knowledge of the process and see if they can follow it; they don't need to understand the technical aspects just be able to follow the process.

Make sure you have defined clearly who is responsible for the process. Often there is more than a single person responsible, if this is the case define who is responsible for which aspects or elements of the process. Without clearly defining these responsibilities, it will be impossible to maintain accountability.

Next you need to setup key performance indicators (KPI) to enable measurement of the system. The best measures are lead indicators. These are measures that indicate an issue or off track target before the system gets off track. It can be difficult sometimes to come up with lead indicators, in these instances we have what are called lag indicators. Lag indicators are still measures and they can be effective to a degree, however as the name suggests these will not indicate an issue until the measure is already off track. A combination of both lag and lead indicators provides the best opportunity to manage the system.

There are three reasons why we utilise KPI's. Firstly, we can use the KPI's to measure the individual performance of those with responsibilities for the process without micro managing. Secondly, we can measure the performance of the system. And thirdly, we can manage the system; by manage the system I mean making decisions and reacting to what the KPI's are telling us.

What are good KPI's for a TPM program?

- OEE is the obvious KPI used to measure the effectiveness of a TPM program. This can be quite a high level indicator as it requires data from many different parts of the business to calculate. You will also require some lower level KPI's that can be utilised faster. In fact you can use the same indicators that feed into the OEE.

  o Machine uptime and availability

  o Throughput

  o Defects

  o Adherence to schedule

  o Operating costs

- Along with the more general system measures

  o Adherence to maintenance schedule

  o Adherence to maintenance budget

  o Frequency of breakdowns

Identify the best combination of these KPI's (and others) for your circumstances and to provide qualitative and quantitative analysis.

Now you have the system developed it is time to put together the schedule. With the information collected in the earlier steps this shouldn't take too long.

For a basic, effective schedule I have found Excel or similar a good choice. In the left column, list all of the equipment. On the top row, run the operating dates – if you only operate Monday to Friday then only add these dates; if you operate 7 days then add all of these dates. Don't include public holidays etc. It can be a good idea to include a staff calendar to keep track of resource availability in the same place.

It can be a good idea to hyperlink the equipment names in the left column to detailed worksheets behind the schedule. These worksheets can include maintenance requirements, frequencies, equipment utilisation and other important information.

In the second column add the priority ranking from earlier. This is useful to make decisions on the run, especially between more than one piece of equipment with limited resources.

In the next couple of columns, define the time requirements for different service types for all of the equipment. This time should be decimals of hours e.g.1.5 hrs = 90 mins. Now in the row below the dates add the available resources in the same format for each day e.g. with 2 staff, each working 7.6 hrs this will be written as 13.2 hours. With some conditional formatting, you can now set up the cells in the available resource row to change colour based on resources required for each column.

Next enter the resource name or number (staff members) into each corresponding cell for equipment and maintenance requirement. Make sure not to over commit the available resources. This can take some time to complete, however the benefits can be great. Like most systems, the more effort in the early stages the better the outcome.

Once complete, the schedule should be printed large (A1 or A0) and posted in the visual management area of the department.

This poster now becomes the work program, leave calendar and resource analysis tool all in one and with a little more work can also be linked (in the electronic file) to the budgets to keep track of maintenance costs against budget.

The information collected earlier can also be used to setup a system for consumables stock holding. One of the biggest wastes I see in maintenance departments is the over and under stock on hand of consumables and spares. These two (consumables and spares) will be discussed separately.

Consumables

Firstly what are consumables? Consumables are items that by design require replacement at some interval. This design can be through running empty as in ink cartridges or through wear and tear as in the replaceable drum in a laser printer.

In the earlier chapters you will have compiled a list of consumables for all of your equipment. Along with this information the manuals will also detail the rate of replacement for these parts. You should have an good idea of the utilisation and therefore the forecast use of the equipment. With this information you can calculate the monthly consumption of all required consumables for your equipment. Now depending on your usage you may be in a position to discuss a service agreement with a supplier to provide a supply or consignment service. If your usage isn't high enough to warrant this you can still control your stock holdings.

By setting minimum stock levels based on your usage versus stock availability with the following formula.

Minimum Stock = S

Monthly Usage = M

Lead Time (Days) = T

Working Days = D

Economic Order Qty - Q

$$S=Q+((M/D)T)$$

Many practitioners also suggest setting maximum stock holdings. This is only necessary if you have an automatic supply setup with your supplier. If the minimum level is adhered to and used as a trigger to purchase the set amount, a maximum level is not required.

Economic Order quantity (EOQ) and lead time are two values that are controlled largely by your supplier. EOQ is determined by how much you are willing to pay to receive your goods. With many suppliers there will be discounts for bulk purchases; this could also be described as paying a premium for smaller lot sizes. Work with your suppliers to agree to terms that are win – win for both parties. By setting up a service agreement you can agree to a medium to long term supply at a good price with low minimum order quantities to reduce the EOQ and shorter lead times. This type of agreement will enable you to hold reduced stock of these items in your stores thereby improving cash flow.

Stock of spare parts is a different proposition. An analysis needs to be undertaken of a number of criteria:

- Age and past service history of the equipment
- Condition of equipment
- Machine utilisation / hours of use per month
- Availability of parts
- Accessibility of available parts
- Cost of replacement parts

Obviously for older equipment and equipment in a worse condition you will need to carry a greater variety and quantity spare parts. This also applies to equipment with higher usage.

When spare parts are easily available and have quick and easy accessibility the requirement to carry stock of spare parts will be reduced. Conversely, where availability is low or difficult to obtain stock requirements will increase.

Cash-flow plays a critical part in managing a business. To have cash tied up with expensive spare parts sitting in the stores could have a negative impact on the daily operations of the organisation. While it is important to have access to spare parts this must be balanced with the impact on cash-flow; to achieve this put in place suppliers and systems to manage the more expensive spare parts.

To analyse all of the above a simple matrix can be used. With one axis measuring the need to hold stock (i.e. age, condition and utilisation if equipment) and the other axis measuring the availability, accessibility and cost of the spare parts. The below diagram shows an example.

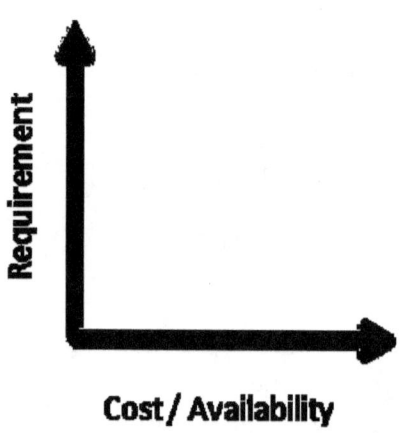

Items sitting in the higher requirement and lower cost/availability bracket are the items you should consider stocking. Items sitting in the higher cost/availability bracket are the items you should set in place a plan or system to enable the supply of spare parts as required. It will become more difficult when there are parts with high cost and low availability. In some instances it will be necessary to put in place alternative processes or process supply while spare parts can be obtained. Demand needs to be weighted in this analysis to ensure the day to day operations of the business are not interrupted.

To create a system that is easily managed and maintained the use of effective visual management is highly recommended. This can be deployed for the program, machine availability as discussed earlier; this will enable the management to be more effective. Visual management can also be deployed to manage the consumable and spares stock holding and usage.

Minimum stock levels as discussed earlier can be managed with visual management, we can go further by visually identifying the consumable items to make restocking and identifying out of stock items faster and easier. Further to this a simple chart can be used in situ to identify changes to usage trends of consumables and spares quickly rather than waiting for data to feed from the systems.

Going to the next level, visual management can help drive accountability by identifying trends in increased parts usage. This can be further analysed to identify the root causes and develop countermeasures. With problem solving occurring at the source of the problem with the people who know the problem best, fast and accurate solutions can be applied. Often, by only having visual management in place we see a substantial improvement in performance. By measuring, analysing and challenging the performance we are driving accountability. By managing with data, there is no argument, either the performance is acceptable (targets met) or it isn't acceptable (targets not met); without spoken words, staff know how they are performing and will often improve without any other changes made.

A quick search on the internet provide plenty of example of visual management used for TPM purposes.

5 – Ground Maintenance

Even with a sustainable TPM program in place, we still require ground level maintenance or preventive maintenance running to ensure the day to day tasks are performed. It can be argued that a preventive maintenance regime is part of the TPM system; I disagree and I'll explain why.

TPM is about ensuring the equipment is effectively maintained to enable productivity to continue as required. Just about every machine in a factory and many machines in office environments have start-up, shutdown or regular requirements for small maintenance tasks. These tasks do not require the skills of a technician, engineer or qualified repairer to perform so can easily be performed by the user or operator of the equipment. This is what preventive maintenance is about.

Sounds easy, it still needs to be managed however. This can be achieved in a number of ways.

The most ineffective method is to leave the onus purely on the operators to perform the preventive maintenance with little process management. For obvious reasons this method is not recommended unless a) you only have equipment that is of the most basic design and ease of use.; or b) you are hoping to close down very soon and are just waiting for our equipment to stop working. Obviously (b) was a joke, but it does show what the worst case scenario of following this method could be. Unfortunately many organisations actually are following this method and then are bewildered when their repairs costs are too high. This would be no different to purchasing a new car, driving out of the sales yard and never again checking the water level, oil level, tyres, battery, belts etc. unless a scheduled service was due. Whilst with most modern cars this would be fine as technology in engines and lubricants has improved; if your driving is in dusty conditions or the engine is under constant heavy load (towing) you may end up with expensive repair bills. My last car was 11 years old when it was damaged beyond cost effective repair in hail storm (we get big hail stones here in Australia); because I consistently performed preventive maintenance between services that car didn't breakdown once and I never had to replace anything more than a gasket or starter motor in its life time.

The next method is to put up signage or instruction of some type. This is where most organisations are with their preventive maintenance systems. In the opinion of management, they are doing things right and giving the staff the tools to perform the tasks required to ensure the equipment remains in good operating condition. However this method is likely to end once again with equipment in need of major repair or replacement (the timing is likely to be much later than with the first method), management will be scratching their heads and blaming staff for not following the instructions, the staff will be blaming the management because they weren't told to do anything; they saw the instructions but thought they were meant for someone else. So the end result is we have equipment that is broken down and low morale from operators to management. This is similar to the situation is many households with whitegoods, vacuum cleaners and the like; how many of us follow the maintenance schedule that come with our washing machines and other white goods? Most do not and many then complain when they break down just outside of the warranty period. I wonder how much longer these would last if we'd followed the maintenance instructions? While this method will provide operational savings over the first method, it's is still not recommended to be followed unless you have a highly technically qualified workforce who have a strong understanding of machine maintenance.

The third and recommended method uses the work started in the second method and takes it much further. Good preventive maintenance instructions will be part of the operating procedure. The two formats for procedures are Standard Operating Procedures (SOP) and Standard Work Instructions (SWI). These can be explained as follows:

Standard Operating Procedure:

These are operating instructions for the equipment. While they can be specific to a process they do not vary by product or volume.

SOP's will usually include start-up and shutdown procedures along with preventive maintenance requirements.

Standard Work Instruction:

Similarly to SOP's these are work instructions, however are more specific to product and process and therefore do vary by product and volume.

SWI's usually include product specification and quality requirements with inspection frequencies etc.

From the above descriptions it is clear that SOP's are the correct documentation format to include the preventive maintenance requirements. Most equipment in the office environment would not require an SWI as they are used for a single process; this equipment should still have an SOP in place.

For this method to be effective we need to manage it. To manage the system we first need to measure it. In order to measure it we need to start recording the start-up checks and maintenance performed. We do this by locating a log book at each machine (next to the SOP is a good place). At this point we have two of the three requirements to ensure this method is successful - good instructions and means to record the actions as they occur. We are missing the third and most important requirement – we still are not measuring anything. How many times have you seen a log book on or next to a machine that is years old, covered in grease with a last entry dated years ago? Without a way to measure what is happening we really are no better off than method two and barely better off than method one.

The data in the log books now becomes one of your lead indicators for your entire TPM system. This data can be measured and analysed on the visual management board to verify the preventive maintenance is having an impact on the overall costs, efficiency and machine availability.

Your preventive maintenance is both a separate system and a part of the same system as your TPM. It is separate as different teams perform and manage the actions to the TPM system yet it is also the same as the outputs and outcomes align.

6 – Maintenance Team Duties

We have discussed the TPM system and we've discussed the preventive maintenance, now we need to define what services of the maintenance team. Not all organisations have a dedicated maintenance team and not all organisations need one; however all organisations need to be smart about how they manage their maintenance. If you don't require a dedicated maintenance team you can still learn from this chapter; if you need but don't have a dedicated team, then I strongly advise doing what you can to change this first.

Outsourcing is an option, and while this can be an expensive option in some circumstances it may actually be a cost effective option; particularly if there is a requirement for expensive specialised equipment to perform the maintenance tasks. If this is the method you decide on for your TPM resourcing I strongly recommend following the TOM system and the preventive maintenance programs discussed earlier in this book. In fact, it is probably more important to follow this system if you are outsourcing than if you're performing the TPM tasks in-house!

So assuming you require and have a dedicated maintenance team let's discuss what it is they should be doing. With the preventive maintenance program in the last chapter it was clear that the operators would be performing what tasks they can, both physically and technically. If there are preventive tasks that require the technical skills of the maintenance team these must be detailed on the SOP's and added to the log books and measurement system. These are likely to be regular activities conducted, so it is important the team have resources available when required. Remember, production is the critical activity of the business (in most cases) and needs to be supported (TPM – Total Productive Maintenance). The number focus of the maintenance team needs to be keeping machinery and equipment operational to enable production. Just like design, finance, customer service, purchasing and others, maintenance is a support business unit.

These regular tasks should be programmed on the TPM schedule as with the less frequent activities, to ensure the resources are available and to give management all of the relevant information.

As with all other departments it is important for the maintenance team to work efficient. The team has to have medium to long term actions to develop the unit and ensure the long term sustainability of the unit. These actions should be part of the business unit strategy and annual plans. These plans should be aligned to the overall organisational strategy and need also need to be added to the TPM schedule.

So the overall time management of the team is through the TPM schedule, however there needs to be weekly and daily activity lists to be followed by the teams. These will be filled with the unplanned maintenance activities that come into the team. Even with the very best TPM systems there will be some unplanned maintenance requests. A system needs to be developed to manage these requests; I would suggest something that considers the following:

- All requests should come through a single channel

    - I recommend making the coordinator or team leader responsible for this

- Use a works ticket system that contains the following:

    - The name of the person requesting the work

    - A detailed description of the problem and the required work

    - The priority for the work. These needs to be based on the impact to the production system due to unplanned downtime

    - The date and time of the request

- A measurement system should be developed to monitor all of the above requirements are being adhered to

When the work requests come into the maintenance team they need to be prioritised as a matter of urgency, depending on the frequency of requests this may to be managed electronically. Obviously the requests that have a greater impact on the production system should be dealt with first, however it is also critical to monitor the timeliness of service to the less urgent requests otherwise these will soon become urgent and will cause delays to production. Just as with any other service unit, the schedule will need to be planned and managed to enable effective and timely delivery. Better planning **always** provides better results.

7 - Next steps

For this and any system to be effective it must align with other critical systems across the organisation. This may seem like stating the obvious but it is amazing how many organisations get this wrong. I see some great system being used in departments; yet due to a lack of integration the potential is not achieved. Each of these functions have interactions that are critical not only to the departments success but to the greater success of the organisation.

For maintenance, these interactions are with:

- Production planning
  - o For medium term machine availability
- Production management
  - o For short term machine availability and repairs
- Finance
  - o For medium to long term asset management
- Sales and Marketing
  - o Utilisation of forecasting models
- Design and Development
  - o To assure capabilities develop to support new innovations

The role of maintenance is often undervalued within an organisation. This will almost always lead to:

- Frustrated maintenance team members

- Low morale

- Higher staff turnover

- Increased team management costs

- Reduced team effectiveness

- Ultimately, increased costs to organisation

An organisation wide strategy needs to be in place to set out the methods, frequencies and expectations from these communications. Measurements will need to be developed to ensure these communications are effective in meeting the expectations.

While on the subject of strategies, it is a good idea to develop a service agreement or charter from the maintenance department. This should detail not only what the department will deliver, but also how, when and why it will be delivered. Instead of just listing the tasks undertaken why not include the outcomes (long term benefits) that these tasks lead to. This document should include:

- What will be delivered from the service

- What are the outcomes from these deliverables

- When and how will the service be delivered

- Service boundaries – where do the maintenance team responsibilities start and end

- What are the responsibilities of others

- Expectations of others

- How will we measure our effectiveness

This document should be signed off by the entire team; this also needs to be signed off by the supplier and customer managers; to assure buy in from all managers.

The keys to this system being effective include:
- Get senior management on board from the beginning
  - Senior management need to be exposed to TPM success stories so they can become believers
- Get the major stakeholders on board
- Sell the truth – TPM is not going to make more work for anyone
  - It's about planning and making the work you do more effective
- The system will need to be managed. More so in the initial stages
- Visual management is a core component of TPM
- Team buy-in
- The system must be resourced

Of this list, senior management buy-in and resourcing the system are the most critical. With senior management on board, many of the other requirements "just happen" as people will follow what they see. Resourcing is often a major struggle to an effective TPM program. While a system of this type will provide tangible long term financial benefits (if implemented successfully), there will need to be a reallocation of resources (both people and financial) in the short term. For those organisations that have successfully implemented this system the results are obvious; it can be difficult however for management and accountants to "see" the benefits in a system unless they have observed first hand how effective a system is. I guess it is a leap of faith to some extent.

Trialling of this type of program can be an option. If the resources cannot be pulled together initially for a full system, you can run a managed program in a selected area with reduced resource requirements. This will enable the required evidence to be collected to prove the value of such a system.

Appendix C

What is a Lean Business?

It is probably best to first explain what a lean business is not. Most businesses (even some that are seemingly fairly successful) are not operated in a lean way. The term lean can be quite confusing and can give business owners and managers the wrong idea.

Many businesses that attempt to operate in a lean way tend to take the title "Lean" and try to operate their business with lean resources. If this occurs during or after running some lean manufacturing programs or kaizen events then the results will invariably a halt or even reversal of progress made through the lean initiatives - this is due to the overburden of labour resources. This can be equally detrimental in a manufacturing or office environment.

What does a lean business really look like?

A lean business is one that has or is in the process of identifying the following traits:

- Has a well defined strategic / business plan

- Has a very clear understanding of its current processes throughout the business

- Has a strong understanding of what its customers define "value adding"

- Understands how all of its internal processes add value to its customers

- Has defined a future state for all internal processes to remove any non-value adding processes

- Has identified gaps between the current and future states

- Has a clear action plan for all gaps

- Has communicated all of the above to internal and external stakeholders

- Has resourced the program and resulting action plan

Every one of the above are important for the successful implementation of a sustainable lean program. Obviously not all will be in place fro the beginning, however without the last one it will be very difficult to attain most of the others.

So to sum up; obviously to even set the program in motion you will need management with some foresight, understanding and desire to achieve success through the implementation of a lean program. However if asked what is the single most important factor in achieving a successful & sustainable lean business, my answer would be "sufficient resources".

This answer is the opposite of the reality seen in so many businesses. So rather than reducing resources each time an efficiency gain is made (to make sure everyone is working 100 - 110% on their core role) change that mindset so your employees are working 80% on their core role and 20% on further lean initiatives.

Appendix C

How Do You Measure?

Measuring the outputs of a process or service may seem like quite an easy thing to do. Unfortunately many organisations get this wrong. What is the impact of getting this wrong? Read on...

Recently I undertook some consultancy work for a Local Government department. They had a problem delivering a certain service within the regulatory timeframes for many years. They were required to report the performance of this service both to the community through their annual report and also to the State Government. The poor results had been under high scrutiny for many years and many internal reviews and improvement projects had been undertaken. While there had been significant improvements, the outputs remained consistently below the targets (which were quite low).

When I was requested to review the process the first action was to define the problem. Now this seemed quite easy and together with the Manager and Team Leader we put together a problem definition statement along the lines of meeting the KPI targets and quality outputs. On the first day of actually reviewing and challenging what I was seeing, it became quite apparent that the data being used to populate the reports was in fact questionable at best. They had a problem with the data integrity!

I decided to collect some evidence of what I suspected. Over the next two weeks I collected my own data to compare with the official data. Not to my surprise there was significant difference. It turned out that on many occasions the process had in fact met or exceeded the targets. One of the major problems was in fact with the data collection and integrity rather than the process. There were concerns over the process, however without first having a reliable data collection and reporting method it was impossible to measure the impact of any improvements.

There are two morals to this story.

1. Measure the right things in the right way

2. The problem definition should be more than a perceived problem. Challenge your PDS through root cause analysis